CHILDREN'S COGNITIVE ENHANCEMENT PROGRAM:

COMBINED LEVELS
REVISED EDITION

Kenneth Kohutek, Ph.D. & Ann Marie Kohutek, Ed. S.

Illustrated by:

David Orenday & Andrea Izaguirre

Library of Congress Cataloging-in-Publication Data

ISBN-13: 978-0-9891164-4-2

To learn more about CCEP or purchase products, visit www.kennethkohutek.com.

Printed in the United States of America

Introduction

This manual was designed to provide school-aged children an opportunity to enhance cognitive skills. Cognitive skills, or "thinking" as more commonly known, are required for an individual to be successful in both the academic and social arenas. There is mounting evidence suggesting that before competencies in language or mathematics can be acquired, development of cognitive skills, such as attention, memory, planning and self-monitoring are crucial. (Students with learning difficulties may be experiencing under developed cognitive skill sets. Thus cognitive skills must be included when developing a Response to Intervention Plan.)

While problem-solving skills are often taught in the classroom setting, there remains a need for students to acquire these skills in a manner where explicit practice can occur. Too often the importance of developing these skills get convoluted with the importance of content mastery. Therefore, the challenges in this manual are specifically designed not to target content mastery. The abilities to plan, monitor, and evaluate one's actions in a systematic fashion are equally, if not more, important in the child's future than content mastery. It is with these goals in mind that this program has been developed. In light of the accelerated speed of information, being able to formulate a plan based on the most current information will require excellent problem-solving skills.

This manual is the combination of the Primary and Elementary Levels manuals. The Combination Manual is intended to be used with students who might benefit from both manuals and/or for those seeking additional enhancement.

The model for this program includes an adult working alongside the child throughout each session. Consequently, in order to gain maximum benefit from the program, a "guide" is strongly recommended. At the beginning of each Level, as well as embedded within the pages, are notes to the guide. This person may be a parent, teacher, or older sibling who understands the process described in the manuals. The guide's responsibilities include providing verbal and physical scaffolding cues as well as providing positive reinforcement as the child advances. Included within the scaffolding cues are "thinking aloud" opportunities where either the student describes the strategy to successfully complete the task or the guide provides verbal cues by "thinking aloud" to assist in training the student in effective problem-solving. It is also the guide's responsibility to be sure each challenge is completed correctly. Hence, the guide is encouraged to be familiar with the manual and challenges on each level. Because the challenges (and strategies) build on previous sessions, it is recommended that the same guide work consistently with the student. (The notes to the guide are meant to be suggestions and not standardized instructions to be read to each child on each page.)

The overall format of this program may appear to not take advantage of available technology. That observation is correct! Children have been taught skills by fellow human beings for countless generations and because technology may remove the "need" for "human" interaction in some instructional process it does not necessarily indicate that it is the most effective method of instruction for some skills.

This program is NOT a one-day project but a project to be spread out over several sessions, often 6 to 8 occurring weekly or bi-weekly. Duration of individual sessions, usually ten to thirty minutes, depends upon the student's ability to focus and gain mastery of the task at hand. Should the child appear distracted or have difficulty focusing on a given day, refer to the Yellow Book or defer the session to another time or day. Often the sessions end after the student has successfully completed a Level. However, gaining mastery of a strategy is more important than completing a level and, should a level not be completed, subsequent sessions can be used. It is the guide's decision to determine the duration and total number of sessions. The above mentioned time frames are recommendations and not specific guidelines. There are seemingly an infinite number of books, software and peer-reviewed journal articles describing various portions of the strategies/constructs addressed in this manual. Topics which may interest the reader include: executive functioning, attention, concentration, memory, metacognition, cognitive skills, problem solving, inductive reasoning, scaffolding, Zone of Proximal Development, or the "Construction Zone" of instruction.

For additional information the following list is provided. Note this list is not meant to be exhaustive.

Barkley, R. (2012). Executive Functions: What they are, how they work and why they evolved. New York: Guilford Press.

Bondrova, E. & Leong, D. J. (2007). Tools of the mind: The Vygotskian approach to early childhood education (2nd ed.). Upper Saddle River, N. J.: Pearson Education, Inc.

Feuerstein, R., Feurstein, R.S. & Falik, L.H. (2010). Beyond Smarter: Mediated learning and the brain's capacity for change. New York: Teachers College Press.

Gathercole, S.E. & Alloway, T.P. (2008). Working Memory and Learning: A practical guide for teachers. London: Sage.

Kohutek, K. (2013). The Children's Cognitive Enhancement Program: A pilot study. *Journal of Scholastic Inquiry: Education, 1(1),* 165-174.

Wertsch, J.V. (1985). Vygotsky and the social formation of mind. Cambridge, Mass.: Harvard University Press.

Young, B. A. & Doide, N. (2012). The woman who changed her brain: And other inspiring stories of pioneering brain transformation. New York: Free Press.

TABLE OF CONTENTS

LEVEL A

FOR THE GUIDE

Level A is the basic level where the student becomes familiar with the format and challenges found in this manual. It begins with very basic patterns for which the solutions are obvious. The student is required to recognize and complete patterns by drawing a line from the correct response to the empty box. After the initial challenges, the format changes to include letters, number, and mixtures of animals, letters and numbers. It is not necessary for the student to be familiar with the alphabet or numbers in order to master the remaining challenges because the emphasis remains on training the student to search for and complete patterns.

The challenges are usually enjoyable and challenging making it relatively easy to keep the student motivated during these sessions. Maintaining motivation and a sense of accomplishment is assured because the guide (you) is working with the student and demonstrating the consistency in developing a strategy and maintaining the strategy throughout the challenge. That being said, the guide must watch for frustration or loss of attention to the challenges. Should either of these behaviors be observed, discontinue the session, try the challenges found in the Yellow Book, or postpone the session to a later time or date.

If the student is not able to grasp the concepts, it is the guide's task to "think aloud" (verbalize the process) while the challenge is completed. This union between the guide's scaffolding and student's involvement is the key ingredient in assisting the student to work beyond their current level of reasoning and to the level they are capable of achieving. This process of training goes by different terms in the literature but it is well documented that the ability to enhance a child's cognitive skills beyond their assessed level of functioning has been well documented (review the recommended readings in the Introduction for details of this work).

While rudimentary and perhaps elementary for some repetition at this level is necessary for reinforcing the skills of problem-solving, memory and planning. Repetition is as essential in cognitive training as it is in training for athletic and academic mastery. Rehearsal assist in training the brain and muscles to respond in a specific manner to a specific situation.

A pitfall may be encountered if the student's initial response is inaccurate. The ability to formulate an alternate solution to a challenge is another critical skill in this training process. Should the initial solution prove to be inaccurate, work with the student by asking the student to "think aloud" and share different ways of looking at the challenge. During that time, the guide can offer questions leading to the correct outcome. Note that the strategy is to work with the student and not give the correct answer. Should alternate solutions be difficult for the student to develop, demonstrate the solution through your "thinking aloud" process.

Remember the program is meant to be educational, challenging and enjoyable for both student and guide. The need for both to be "psychologically available" and involved in the process is required for successful completion of this program. The positive findings from research supporting the effectiveness of this program were reported with Guides who were as involved (or more involved at times) in the challenges as the student. **This is NOT a workbook meant to fill time as "busy work"!** So turn the page and get involved in helping shape the problem-solving skills of someone.

As you work through the next few pages, it is important to remember that the guide is providing cues and clues…not reading the suggested prompts verbatim. Finally, you will notice two fonts in the guide sections. One font includes guidelines when talking with the student and the other includes **additional cues or prompts for the guide.**

2

LEVEL A

We are going to look at different challenges and figure out how to solve them. Then we will go to the Yellow Book where there are other kinds of challenges. In both books you will be looking for cues and clues to solve each of these challenges.

In addition to me, your guide, there are others you will find in these pages who will help you. The boy in this book is Joe and he will lead the way. His picture is on the first page of this manual.

There is also Sid the squirrel:

Al the alligator:

Fred the frog:

Bernie the bear:

Charlie the cat:

And

Delbert the dog:

Now let's get started!

Imagine you are a detective and about to solve the challenges in this book. The first thing a detective must do is to look for clues. The clue on this page is that no matching animals can be in the same row or column. For example:

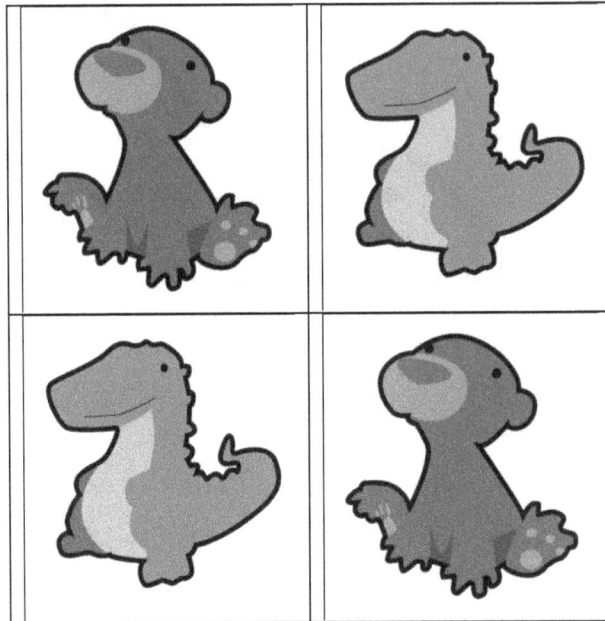

You see that neither the bear nor the alligator are in the same row or column as another bear or alligator. On the next few pages there will be animals in boxes but some boxes are empty and need an animal in it. We will use clues to figure out which animal should be in the empty box.

OR

Look at these rows. You see one bear and one alligator. Then here is an alligator and a bear. When you look at the columns you see a bear and a crocodile, then one alligator and a bear. You never see 2 bears or 2 crocodiles in the same row or column.

You see a dog and a frog on the top row...A dog and a frog in this column...Here there is a frog and an empty box....What animal should go there? Draw a line to where the missing animal belongs.

THAT'S RIGHT! Now draw a line from the dog to the empty box.

EXCELLENT! Let's go to the next page.

Now it is your turn!! See if you can draw a line from the correct animal to the empty space.

(If student struggles, have him/her identify the animals aloud and work through the process by "thinking aloud".)

The line from the dog to the empty box is correct!!

You see a cat and a bear on the top row...A bear and a cat in this column...Here there is a cat and an empty box....What shape should go there?

Remember always look for the empty box and then look at the other boxes for the clues to tell you what should be in the empty box. Now what goes in this empty box? Draw a line from the animal to the empty box.

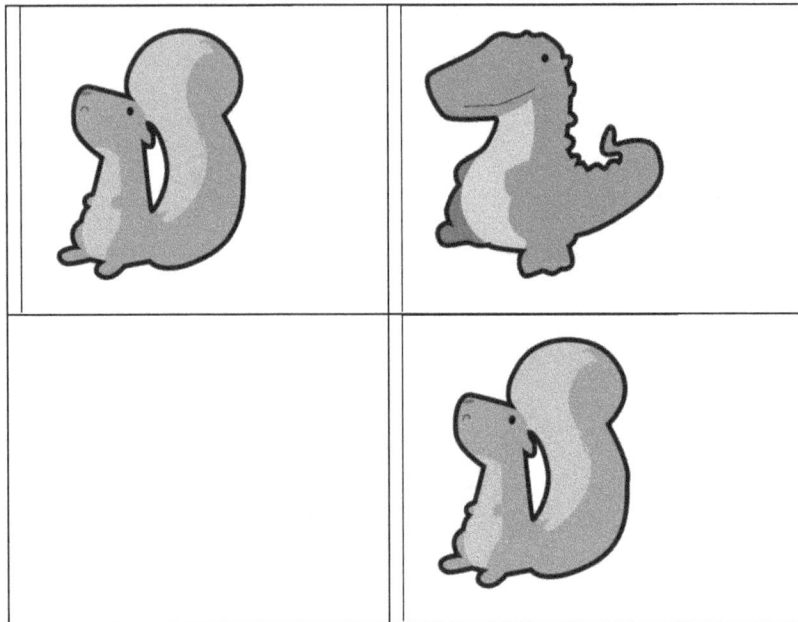

THAT'S RIGHT! Now draw a line from the alligator to the empty box......EXCELLENT! Let's go on to the next page.

Now here....draw a line from the missing animal to the empty box.

Draw a line from the missing animal to the empty box.

Tell me what should be in this empty box. Now draw a line from that animal to the empty box.

Tell me how you are going to solve this puzzle.

How would you complete this challenge?

On this page are three different animals, but keep doing the same thing! Draw a line from the missing animal to the empty box.

If student struggles, say "name the animals aloud and point out patterns..cat, bear, frog...bear, frog, cat...and so on.

(If answers incorrectly or does not know, provide with the below multiple choices.)

Should it be the cat? Is there a cat in that row?
Is there a cat in that column?

The bear? Is there a bear in that row?
Is there a bear in that column?

The frog? Is there a frog in that row?
Is there a frog in that column?

How about this one?

How would you complete the challenge on this page?

We can do the same thing with letters. Look at the pattern. There is only one of each letter in each row and column.

A	B	C
B	C	A
C	A	B

What letter should be in the empty box?

A	B	C
B		A
C	A	B

A   B   C

(If student struggles, read the letters pointing out pattern.) "Look at each complete line. It has an A, B, and C. What goes here?"

Do the same thing here.

A	C	
B	A	C
C	B	A

A   B   C

Do this one the same way. This time write the missing letter in the empty box.

B	C	A
A	B	C
C	A	

Prompting might include: "Could it be an A, or do we already have an A in this row and column? How about a B? Does this row and this column have a B? Does each row/column need a B? Yes, then a B goes there. Now does each row/column have a C? Yes..

Perfect!!!!

This time there are two empty boxes and two missing letters but there are still patterns and it can be solved the same way. Write the correct letters in the empty boxes.

	C	A
A	B	C
C	A	

Possible Prompts: Is there any row or column that is completely filled in? That is our first clue. Row 2 has "A..B..C", Column 2 has "C..B..A"..we know every row and column should have the same 3 letters. Now we know we need an A, B, and a C for each row and column. Let's look at this row. There is a "C" and here is an "A". What is missing? What is needed to complete the pattern?

It is possible for there to be both letters AND animals in the same challenge. We are still looking at patterns even though the designs in the boxes change.

A		B
B	A	
	B	A

What letter or animal belongs in the empty box on this page?

A	C	
		C
C		A

Possible Prompt: "Tell me what is in each box aloud..both by row, then column..A..C.. alligator..A...alligator...C..Now here is an alligator, a blank space and a C..What is missing from this line?"

26

What is missing from this challenge?

C	A	
A		C
	C	A

This time there are two empty boxes. But there is a pattern. How would you solve this challenge?

A		
B		
	B	A

Here is another with two empty boxes. How are you going to solve this challenge?

C	A	B
B		A
	B	C

Possible Prompts: What clues do you have? Are there any rows complete? Any columns complete? Do you know all three letters? What is missing from column 1? How about column 2?

There can also be letters and numbers in the boxes. What needs to be added to complete the page?

B	C	1
	B	C
C	1	B

Possible prompts: Are there any rows/columns complete? These are your clues to start with. What is in row 1? Row 3? Column 2? And column 3? Since all rows and columns need the same three items what is missing?

Again...what do you know? What are your clues?

A	C	
1	A	C
C	1	A

How would you complete the challenge on this page?

B	C	
	B	
C		

POSSIBLE PROMPTS: What are your clues? Do you have any rows complete? Do you have any columns complete? Do you know what 3 things have to be in each row and column?

What is missing from this challenge?

B		
	B	A
A		

POSSIBLE PROMPTS: What are your clues? Look at your complete rows and columns before you fill in the empty boxes.

Now there are letters, numbers and animals. This can be solved the same way. The three things in the boxes include the letter "C", the number "1" and a "frog", What would you need to put in each box to complete this challenge?

		C
		1
C	1	

Have the student look for completed rows or columns first to "see" what they are looking for. If they struggle have them say "aloud" what is in each completed row or column.

Now complete this challenge.

2	A	
A		2

POSSIBLE PROMPTS: Again have the student look for clues! "Are there any completed rows/columns. What does each completed row/column have? What is missing from column 2? What is missing from column 3?"

**Point out that it is easier to solve column 2 and then 3 instead of row 2 because of the number of empty boxes. It is easier to find one missing item than two in a line.

Once again...complete this challenge.

This time there are numbers and alligators with three empty boxes. Use the same strategy for finding the clues and you will be able to solve this one.

POSSIBLE PROMPTS: "Let us look for clues. Are there any completed rows or columns? What are the three things you need?...a "2".. an alligator...a "1". Find a row or column that has only one empty box. What is missing? Now find another row or column that is missing only one empty box What is missing?.. Now there should be only one empty box. What is missing?"

Tell me how you would solve this one.

1		
	1	A

POSSIBLE PROMPTS: "Let's look for clues. Are there any complete rows or columns? What three things do you need for each row and column?

YEAH!!!!!

YOU finished this part of Level A and can go to the Yellow Manual.

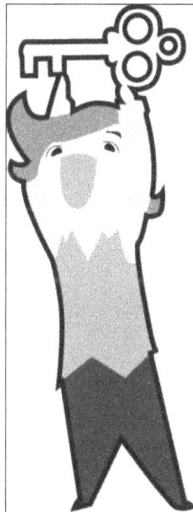

LEVEL 1

FOR THE GUIDE

The student will continue to be encouraged to search for patterns and use that information in solving the challenges on this Level. These challenges increase in difficulty in that numbers, rather than animals or letters, are utilized. Also, the number of empty boxes increases as progress is made through this level.

Key cognitive skills addressed include <u>planning</u>, <u>attention</u>, and <u>memory</u>. Planning is the most important skill with scaffolding being the primary factor in the student-guide interaction. At the onset, detailed instructions are presented. As the student settles into a routine, it is recommended that the oral instructions be reduced. (It has been noted that students will often work with the guide in developing strategies consistent with their problem-solving abilities. However, as the guide begins to fade out the instructions, the student may revert to more random patterns of attempting to complete the challenge. Hence, the guide may need to provide frequent reminders of formulating a plan before trying to solve the challenge). This process of planning will increase in importance as the challenges on this Level, and subsequent Levels, become more difficult. Bringing planning to the conscious level is the most important skill addressed during this Level.

Both <u>attention</u> and <u>memory</u> will become a part of the program as the challenges become more complex. Focused attention to the challenge and the steps to successfully complete that challenge remain important. Sustained attention is required because the challenges become more difficult and increase in number. Attention may be an issue with younger students, as well as older students who experience difficulty focusing or completing an assignment. These exercises provide an excellent opportunity to increase the ability to focus. **The guide must stay attuned to the disposition of the student and his/her ability to successfully engage in the task**. It is important to discontinue the task prior to the student refusing to continue. A statement like, "Let's stop here today" or "Let's work on the challenges in the Yellow Book" will keep some students engaged for the next session.

The <u>memory</u> component is a key in that both the rules for mastering the challenge, as well as the proper placement of numbers on the page are critical. Asking the student to "think aloud" before and during completion of the challenges will assist in enhancing memory skills. Initially thinking aloud may seem awkward to the child because that behavior is often discouraged in the classroom. Nevertheless, sharing the planning process is an important part of these exercises and should be encouraged.

It is not necessary to complete a level during one sitting. After five or ten minutes, depending on the student, most students will gain mastery of the task. At that time, move on to the Yellow Book with plans to return to this challenge during the next session. This approach allows for incremental learning, rather than massed practice. This process has found that many students returning to a previously practiced strategy require minimal, or no, assistance in picking up where left off.

Finally, it is likely that a strategy may be verbalized which would lead to an incorrect solution. If this situation occurs, it may be necessary to intervene by asking if there are other strategies to solve the challenge. The key at this time is for the guide to lead the student to the correct solution, not to solve the challenge! Should the student insist on implementing a solution which is incorrect, allow the solution to be implemented and then question its accuracy (such as "Can you have more than one '2' in a row or column?"). It is often much easier to correct an error after it is placed on paper and the student visualizes the error. Once more it is emphasized that the instructions to the guide found on these pages are guidelines and may be altered to fit the skill level of the student.

LEVEL 1

For the next few minutes we are going to solve number puzzles. The rules are the same as the picture and letter puzzles! Each puzzle should have all of the boxes filled with no number appearing twice going across (row) or up and down (column). An example of a completed puzzle is on this page.

1	2	3
2	3	1
3	1	2

Have student read through each row and column aloud.

On the rest of the pages, numbers will be missing from the challenge. You are to find the empty boxes, then using clues put the missing number in the empty spaces.

For example, the following puzzle has one number missing:

1	2	3
2	3	1
3	1	

You see that all of the rows and columns have the number 1, 2, and 3 except the last column which only has 3 and 1. What number should go into the empty box? … If you said "2" you are exactly correct!

LET'S TRY ANOTHER. Look with me. Here is 1, 2, 3 going across (ROW). Going down (COLUMN) is 1, 2, 3. In the middle is 2, 3, 1. Now look —here is a 3 and a 1 . . . what is missing?

REMEMBER -- Each challenge should have all of the boxes filled with no number appearing twice going across (row) or up and down (column).

1	2	3
2	3	1
3	1	

You should be able to solve the rest of these with no problem. All you will need to do is to put on your thinking cap and sniff out the clues with Delbert the guide dog.

REMEMBER. BEFORE YOU START FILLING IN THE BOXES, tell me what number is missing and why it should be put in the empty box. After you tell me what you are going to do, fill in the empty box.

Take a look at this page. You see that in every box whether you go across (row) or up and down (column), there is a 1, 2, and a 3. But one is missing. Let's see...here we have (point) 1,2,3....1,2,3..., 1,2,3 (GUIDE—POINT TO THE CORRECT NUMBERS IN EACH SEQUENCE EVEN THOUGH THEY ARE OUT OF ORDER) and finally <u>blank</u> 2,3. What should be in that empty box?

1	2	3
2	3	1
3		2

(TO THE GUIDE: USE ADDITIONAL PROMPTS IF NECESSARY. IT IS IMPORTANT THAT THE STUDENT GET THIS ACCURATE AS WELL AS KNOW WHY THEIR ANSWER IS CORRECT.)

Now look at this page. You see that in every box whether you go across (row) or up and down (column) there is a 1, 2 and a 3. But one number is missing. Let's see…here we have (point) 1, 2, 3….1, 2, 3… 1, 2, 3 and finally 1, 2, blank. What should be in that empty box?

2	3	1
	1	2
1	2	3

Now this one. Once again, you see a 1, 2 or 3. But one is missing. Let's see...here we have (POINT) 1, 2, 3....1, 2, 3..., 1,2,3 and finally 1, 2, blank. What should be in that empty box?

1	2	3
2	3	1
	1	2

(To The Guide: It is anticipated that many students will begin to recognize the pattern on this page. If so, the instructions can be shortened by asking the student to count the numbers in the rows and columns.)

Now this one. Once again, you see a 1, 2 and a 3. But one is missing. Let's see...here we have (point) 1, 2, 3....1, 2, 3..., 1, 2, 3 and finally 1, blank, 3. What should be in that empty box?

1	3	2
3	2	1
	1	3

(To the Guide: use only the instructions necessary to keep the student going. HOWEVER, make sure they tell you what the steps are and that they count aloud!)

Here we have a picture and one box is empty. What pattern do you see? (Have student point out 1, 2, 3... 1, 2, 3 and so on. You might even direct by asking "What do you see here?" first pointing to rows, then columns). Now put the correct number there.

1		3
2	3	1
3	1	2

(To the Guide: Continue to fade out directions with the student stating the pattern aloud and entering the correct answer.)

Now this one. Count the numbers in the rows as well as the columns. Then tell me what is missing and where it should be.

3	1	2
1	2	3
2		1

You are hopping right through this!

There are two empty boxes but the challenge can be solved the same way. Once again, you see a 1, 2 and 3. Would you count them and then tell me what is missing? ...Now put the numbers where they belong.

2	1	3
3	2	
1		2

(Possible Prompt: Let's look for clues. Are there any completed rows or columns? (YES). What are the three numbers in each completed row or column? Now in the incomplete rows/columns   ..What number is missing?)

1	3	2
3		1
2	1	

Do this the same way. Start by counting the numbers in the boxes, then tell me the numbers that should be in the empty boxes.

2	3	1
1	2	
3		2

You are meowing right along!!!

	3	1
3		2
1	2	3

(PROMPT: What 3 numbers are in each completed row or column?)

How will you solve this one? Tell me first.

	1	2
1		3
2	3	1

Now this one. Tell me your plan before starting.

	2	3
2	3	1
	1	2

YEAH!!!!!

YOU finished this part of Level 1 and can go to the Yellow Manual.

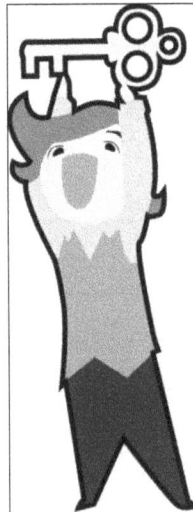

LEVEL 2

TO THE GUIDE

Level 2 is a continuation of Level 1 in that a 3x3 grid remains the challenge. Several of the first items are similar to Level 1. As the challenge progresses, however, additional empty boxes are added. The instructions remain the same except the student should be taking a much more active part in the process. Attention, memory and planning continue to be the skills addressed. Attention is required to complete each challenge and, as the number of challenges per level are increasing, sustained attention becomes more important.

Memory is necessary for each challenge in that the student must remember what numbers are missing as well as the sequence, or order, in which they must be entered. The ability to recall instructions is stretched with the student having to repeat the instructions prior to completing each challenge (This may prove difficult for younger students who may want to start the task prior to completion of their "thinking aloud").

Planning is required when the student is actually able to take time to review the requirements of the challenge and plan successfully. This has proven to be a stumbling block at times because of the desire to engage prior to making a plan. This step is cricital because impulsive actions often prevent the student from conceptualizing the "big picture", thus making unnecessary errors.

There are challenges, similar to that found on page 73, with two empty boxes in the same row or column. This is not a new pattern in that there were similar challenges in Level A. However, when confronted with a more complex task (2 empty boxes) encourage the student to look at a different perspective or to take an easier approach (fill in the row or column that only has one empty box first). Some students will need to be guided in the direction of seeking a number of clues, then using the clue which makes the challenges easier to complete.

Remember, the goal is 100% success. For that to occur, the amount of prompting required will vary with the skill level of the student. This is an example of the student and guide creating the environment where the "Construction Zone" in the "Zone of Proximal Development" is addressed and learning is taking place (also referred to as "Scaffolding").

The rules stay the same on this level. Just keep your thinking hat on and you will do great!!!

Take a good look at this page. You see that in every box whether you look across (row) or up and down (column), there is a 1, 2 or a 3. But one number is missing. Let's see...here we have (point) 1, 2, 3....1, 2, 3..., 1, 2, 3 and finally 1, 2, ____. What should be in that empty box?

1	2	3
2		1
3	1	2

GO!!

Take a good look at this page. Once again, there is a number in every box in each row and column, except for two. Show me where the empty boxes are.... That's RIGHT! Here we have (point) a 1, 2, 3....1, 2, 3..., 1, 2, 3... 1, 2, blank. What would finish that row? Then here is a 2, 3 blank. What should be in that empty box?

1	2	3
2		1
3		2

Now this one! Look for clues. Which line is completely filled in?

(If student does not start by counting the numbers in the boxes prompt by saying 'remember you start by looking and naming what is each box').

	3	
3		2
1	2	3

This time count with me and tell me what should be in the empty boxes.

2	3	1
	1	2
1		3

AWESOME!!

Again... count with me and tell me what should be in the empty boxes.

1	2	3
2	3	
	1	2

You do this one by yourself. Remember to look and say what is in each box before telling me your answers.

1		2
3	2	1
	1	3

You are getting this!

Again...You do it by yourself. Remember to look and say what is in each box before telling me your answers.

3	1	
1	2	3
2		1

keep doing these the same way

There are 3 empty boxes in this puzzle but these can be solved in the same way.

2	1	
3		1
1		2

(PROMPT: Remember look for the row or column that has only one empty box first and fill it in. Then look for another row or column that has only one empty box. You are adding to the clues.)

Now this one. Remember to look and say what is in each box before filling in your answers.

	3	2
3		1
2	1	

Now this one.

	3	1
1	2	
	1	2

Tell me the steps to solving this page.

(IF STUDENT CANNOT TELL YOU....prompt by saying 'remember you start by looking and naming what is each box').

	2	3
2	3	
	1	2

Do this one the same way. There is no line completely filled in here but remember there can only be the numbers 1, 2, or 3.

(If student does not start by counting the numbers in the boxes prompt by saying 'remember you start by looking and naming what is each box').

	1	2
1		3
2	3	

Keep doing these the same as the ones you have already completed.

	2	3
2	3	
	1	2

1		3
2	3	
	1	2

Always start with a plan!!

Do this one the same way!

(If student does not start by counting the numbers in the boxes prompt by saying 'remember you start by looking and naming what is each box').

1		3
2	3	
3		2

What you are supposed to do first? Remember there can only be the numbers 1, 2, or 3.

(If student does not start by counting the numbers in the boxes prompt by saying 'remember you start by looking and naming what is each box').

2		1
	1	
1	2	

(Possible Prompt: pick a row or column with only one empty box. It is easier to solve one problem at a time....not trying to solve two.)

(If student does not start by counting the numbers in the boxes prompt by saying "remember you are still doing a 1, 2, 3 pattern. Pick a row or column with one missing box".)

1		
3		1
	1	3

(Possible prompt: what is missing? ...Fill it in...now find another row or column with one empty box.)

Now this one.

(If student does not start by counting the numbers in the boxes prompt by saying "Remember we are still doing a 1, 2, 3 pattern. Pick a row or column with one empty box".)

	2	3
2	3	
		2

Work this one the same way. Remember the steps.

(If student does not start by counting the numbers in the boxes prompt by saying "what numbers do we have? What is the pattern?)

	1	2
1		3
2		

You are hopping right through these

Keep Going!

(If student does not start by counting the numbers in the boxes prompt by saying "What numbers are missing? What is the pattern?")

2		3
3	2	
	1	

"Tell me what you are supposed to do first?"

(If student does not start by counting the numbers in the boxes prompt by saying "What are the numbers? What is the pattern?")

1	3	2
		1
2		

Now here.

(If student does not start by counting the numbers in the boxes prompt by saying "What numbers are you using? What is the Pattern?")

		1
1	2	
3		2

What are you supposed to do first?

(If student does not start by counting the numbers in the boxes prompt by saying "Remember to ask yourself what numbers am I using? What is the pattern?")

2	3	
	1	
1	2	

Do the same thing on this page.

**(If student does not start by counting the numbers in the boxes prompt by
saying "What numbers am I using? What is the pattern?")**

1		3
		1
	1	2

Keep going!

(If student does not start by counting the numbers in the boxes prompt by saying "remember you start by looking and naming what is each box.")

	2	
1		2
	1	3

You are AWESOME!!!

"First tell me what you are supposed to do. Then solve this challenge."

(If student does not start by counting the numbers in the boxes prompt by saying "What numbers are you using? What is the pattern?").

3		2
1		
2		1

Do the same thing here!

(If student does not start by counting the numbers in the boxes prompt by saying "What numbers are missing? What is the pattern?").

	2	
2	3	
	1	2

YOU FINISHED LEVEL 2!!!!

NOW THE YELLOW BOOK!!

LEVEL 3

FOR THE GUIDE

Level 3 becomes more complex in that there are now 16 rather than 9 boxes in each challenge because the number 4 has been added to the series. The rules for solving the challenges remain the same but the student is required to retain more information in their memory. The student must remember the requirements to successfully complete the challenges as well as the series of numbers in the different rows and columns. The student should be taking more initiative in the process of describing the challenge before starting to complete the task. If this process does not occur without prompting, remind the child the pattern remains the same. Suggested prompts will be provided on the first few pages of this Level but these should fade out as quickly as possible.

Attention, memory and planning continue to be the cognitive skills addressed. However, there is more for the student to focus on and younger students may begin to experience difficulty in this process. If frustration is noted, it is not necessary to continue at this time. Similar to previous levels, memory is stretched. Consequently, reminding the student of the clues as well as the possible choice of numbers may be necessary. Planning continues to be an element to address and the student may also be reminded to "talk aloud" when trying to develop a strategy for each challenge.

Remember, the goal is 100% success. For that to occur, the amount of prompting required will vary by student and challenge. This is a working example of the student and Guide creating the environment where the "Construction Zone" in the "Zone of Proximal Development" is developed.

Strategies to be implemented remain similar to previous levels during the first portion of this Level. As the challenges continue, additional strategies need to be included. For example, there will be rows and/or columns which will have two blank boxes. When that occurs, the student may need to be asked: "What clues are there? What numbers are present and which are not there? Check nearby rows and columns to see if the missing numbers are in those rows or columns." It is through this process of elimination, or searching for clues, that the student will further develop deductive reasoning.

LEVEL 3

The puzzles in this section are different because there are more boxes and numbers but you can solve them in the same way that you solved those on Level 2!!

Be sure to keep your thinking cap on!

First, what is the pattern? 1, 2, 3, 4.....right! Now, locate the row or column which has the fewest empty boxes. Start with that line and work your way through these challenges.

1	2	3	4
2		4	3
3	4	1	
4	3	2	1

Do not be fooled because there are three empty boxes! Look at the rows and columns that are completely filled. What do they all have? (1, 2, 3, 4). Now look for a row or column with only one empty box..Fill in the missing number. Again, go to a row or column with only one empty box. Fill that in first.

	3		2
3		2	4
2	4	3	1
4	2	1	3

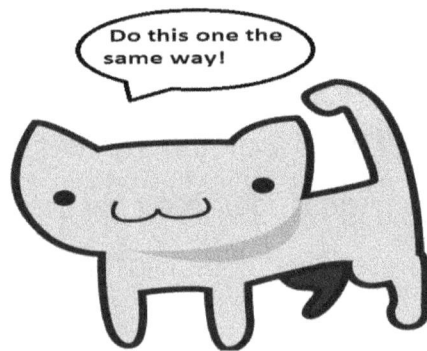

Do this one the same way!

1		2	3
4	2		1
	1	4	2
2	3	1	

Now you tell me what you are going to do in order to complete this challenge.

1	2	3	4
2	1	4	3
	4		
4		2	1

	3		2
3		2	4
2		3	1
4	2	1	

	2	1	4
4	3		1
1		3	
	1		3

Always start with a plan!!

2		1	4
	2	3	
1	4		3
		4	

First look for the row or column with the fewest empty boxes. Start there.

3		1	
	3	2	1
1	4		
2	1	4	3

Now complete this one. Always start with a plan and you will be able to complete all of these challenges !

4	2		1
1	3		4
3		1	2
	1		3

There are more empty boxes but the same rules will help you through these.

3	2		
4			1
1	4	3	
		4	3

Remember first solve for one empty box, then solve for two empty boxes. As you get more clues you may get to go back to solving for one box.

The next few will be a bit tricky. First, look at what do we know? We are still using numbers 1, 2, 3, and 4.

       * First we fill in the rows and columns which have only one empty box.

* Next we see that there are no more rows or columns with only one box missing. So we look for two empty boxes. Looking at the first column we see a 4 and a 1. What two numbers are missing?....2 & 3 right? * Now we have to decide which box gets the 2 and which box gets the 3. Can the first box get the 2? Is there already a 2 in the first row? So it can't be 2 then it has to be 3. If the first box in that column is 3 then where does the 2 go?....Correct!
* Now you are back to having rows one and four with only one empty box. One empty box for you is easy!

	2	1	
4		2	
1	4		2
	1	4	

This is another tricky one. First fill in the row/column with only one empty box. Next, look at a row or column with two empty boxes. Let's look at row one. There is a 3 and 4. So what is missing? ...Yes a 1 and a 2. Now which goes in which box? Can a 1 go in the first box? Is there a 1 in the first column? No. So 1 can go in the first box. Now in row 1 we have a 1, 3, and 4 so the 2 goes in the last box. At this point you can start solving for one empty box per row and column.

	3	4	
3	4		1
2		3	
		1	3

4	2		
3		2	
1		4	2
2	1		4

Where do you start here? .. one empty box in a row/column.

Why?.. it is easier and it gives you more clues.

3	4	1	
1	3		4
		3	1
2	1	4	

Where do you start?

Why?

4	2		
		4	1
1	4		2
3		2	

Where do you start?

Why?

	2	1	3
2			1
1	4		2
3		2	4

Where do you start?
Why?

3	2	4	
2			4
1		3	2
4	1		3

You are hopping right through these

Here we go again. What do you know? Where do you start? Why?

4		1	3
2	3		
		3	2
	1	2	

Where do you start? Why?

3	4	1	2
2	1		4
1	2	4	3
4			1

2		1	
	2		1
1	3		4
		3	

AGAIN!!

119

4		1	
2	4		1
3		4	
1	3		4

2	4		3
1		3	
4	3		1
3		4	

		3	1
4	1		
3		1	4
1	3	4	2

2	1	4	
		3	
3	2	1	4
		2	1

2		1	
	2	4	1
	3		4
4		3	2

1		4	
	4		
2	3	1	4
			2

1		3	4
2			3
	4	1	
4		2	1

YEAH!!!!!

YOU FINISHED LEVEL 3 IN
THIS BOOK!

NOW GO TO THE YELLOW
MANUAL AND COMPLETE
LEVEL 3!!

LEVEL 4

FOR THE GUIDE

There are 20 boxes in each puzzle with the numbers 1 through 5 found in each row/column. There are three strategies which will be reinforced in this level. The first set of strategies are relatively straight forward but must be reinforced frequently for continued success on this and future levels: 1) count the number of blank boxes in each rows/columns; 2) determine the line with the fewest empty boxes; 3) count the sequence (1, 2, 3, 4, 5) to determine which number (s) might be missing; 4) enter the missing number (s); 5) make sure it is compatible with both the row and column in which it is found. When that row/column is complete, the row/column with the next fewer, and so on needs to be solved. To successfully complete this level, the student will need to be aware of the number and location of empty boxes. Once this process is explained, the instructor demonstrates that the sequence 1, 2, 3, 4, 5 can be found consistently in all rows and columns.

The second strategy is initially located on page 146. The four upper boxes in the left hand corner are empty and cannot be completed using the above five steps. Deductive reasoning is very important in solving this challenge. The final strategy on this level will be challenges in which there can be more than one correct solution. The ability to grasp the concept of more than one solution might prove perplexing to some students with the solution needing assistance. The goal for the child is to grasp that the outcome remains the same even as the strategies vary. If a great deal of scaffolding is utilized, it is recommended that the child be encouraged to develop a personal strategy.

The process of solving these challenges will take more time than previous levels. This may lead to frustration in some students. It will be necessary to provide frequent positive feedback (see suggestions on bottom of many pages). Frequent prompts and the watchful eye of the guide monitoring the levels of attention and/or frustration will be most effective.

REMEMBER! IT IS O. K. IF A LEVEL IS NOT COMPLETED IN EACH SESSION!!!

For this level to provide the designed training, it is important that: 1) the guide be aware of the different strategies in this level; 2) the gradual removal of scaffolding as the student internalizes the concepts, and finally; 3) the guide being familiar with the correct strategies and answers to the challenges BEFORE the student is presented the challenge.

Attention, memory, problem-solving/planning as well as the ability to develop an alternate hypotheses should the initial plan not be correct are all necessary for success. Note that attention continues to be required for the student to complete each challenge and there is more information to which the student must attend. Younger students may begin to have difficulty on this level and, if frustration is noted, it is not necessary to continue at this time.

Similar to previous levels, memory is required in that the student must remember which numbers are missing as well as the sequence, or order, in which they must be entered. The ability to recall instructions is stretched with the student having to repeat the instructions prior to completing the task and making a correct decision. This may prove difficult because some students will want to start the task prior to completion of their talking about it. This step is essential for success on future difficult challenges.

It is usually similar impulsive actions that prevent the student from conceptualizing the entire situation and grasping the required material.

Planning/problem-solving is required in that the student is encouraged to take his time to review the requirements of the challenge and successfully complete that page on the first trial. There may be opportunities for the student to reformulate the plan should the initial strategy prove to be inaccurate. If the strategies are followed, however, these opportunities will be minimal. However, when it is discovered that the initial strategy was not the correct one, the student needs to be able to start over or "work backward" in order to develop the correct strategy.

Remember, the goal is 100% success on the initial attempt of each challenge! For that to occur, the amount of prompting required will vary by student. This is an example of the student and instructor creating the environment where the "Construction zone" or the zone of proximal development is addressed and learning is taking place.

LEVEL 4

The challenges in this section require you to be able to determine what numbers are missing in each row and column. After deciding what number, or numbers, may be missing, fill in the empty boxes. The challenges start out easy but they become more difficult as you work your way through the level. There will be clues along the way and the guide will be there to work with you. Remember to take your time and plan a strategy <u>before</u> you begin. Do not start completing the challenges until you have had time to think and make a plan!

Take a good look at this challenge. You see that in every box whether you go up and down or across, there is a 1, 2, 3, 4 or 5. You see in the third column a number box is empty. Let's see…here we have (point) 1, 2, 3, 4, 5….1, 2, 3, 4, 5…, 1, 2, 3, 4, 5 and, 1, 2, 3, 4, 5. Here is the column which has a blank, 2, 3, 4, and 5.What should be in that empty box?

1	2	3	4	5
2	3	5	1	4
3	1	4	5	2
4	5		2	3
5	4	2	3	1

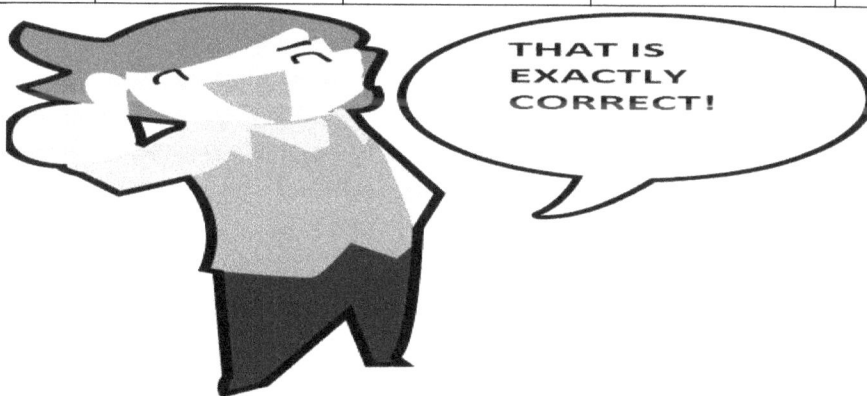

THAT IS EXACTLY CORRECT!

Here you see most boxes have numbers. In every row or column that is complete, you have a 1, 2, 3, 4, or 5. Find a complete line of numbers. Now find a line of numbers that has an empty box. What number is missing? Now find another line of numbers with an empty box. What is missing? You have one more to fill. What number goes there?

1	2	3	4	5
2	3	5	1	4
3	1	4	5	2
4		1	2	3
	4	2		1

Be sure the numbers fit in both the row and column!

Again we are working with 1, 2, 3, 4, and 5. Look across the first row….1, 2, 3, 4, 5, and look at the first column 1, 2, 3, 4, 5. Now find a row or column with an empty box. What numbers does it have? What number is missing? Fill in the missing number. Now find another empty box and do the same thing..figure out what number is missing. You have one more. What number is missing?

1	2	3	4	5
2	3		1	4
3	1	4	5	2
4		1	2	3
5	4	2		1

This challenge has 5 empty boxes. That may seem like a lot but if you look closely you only have one empty box in each row or column. Just take those one at a time and you will do fine. Look across the first row. What numbers do you have? Yes..1, 3, 4, and 5. What is missing? Yes 2. Now look down the second column.

3		5	4	1
1	3	4		5
2	1		5	4
	5	2	1	3
5	4	1	3	

What numbers are already filled in? Yes....1, 3, 4, 5 and you see that the 2 fits in the row AND column.

AWESOME!!

Remember the rules below for success on this Level!

1. Count the number of empty boxes in each row/column;
2. Find the row/column with the fewest number of empty boxes;
3. Count the numbers to find out which number is missing;
4. Put the missing number in the blank box;
5. Make sure the number fits in both the row and column!

DO THIS ONE BY USING YOUR STRATEGIES!!

5	3	4	1	2
2	1		3	4
1	5	2		3
3	4	1	2	5
	2		5	1

You are hopping
right through
these

Count the empty boxes in each row and column. Write the number of empty boxes by that row or column. Start with the line that has the fewest empty boxes.

1	4	3	2	5
5	3	2	1	4
3	1	4	5	
2	5	1		3
4	2	5		

1. Count the number of empty boxes in each row and column.
2. Find the row or column with the fewest number of empty boxes.
3. Count the numbers to discover what number is missing.
4. Put the missing number in the empty box.
5. Make sure the number fits in both the row and column.
   REMEMBER: Each number can only appear once in each row and column.

	1		4	5
1		5		
3	2	4	5	1
4	5			3
5		1	3	2

Remember to start with the row or column with the the fewest missing numbers.

REMEMBER THE STRATEGIES!!!

1		3	5	
4	3			2
3		4	2	5
	5	1	4	3
5	4	2	3	

Guide: Refer to the strategies on page 140 if necessary.

KEEP GOING! There are more empty boxes but the strategy is the same.

	1	3	4	5
4	3		1	
5			3	4
1	5	4	2	
	4	2		1

1. Count the number of empty boxes in each row/column.
2. Find the row/column with the fewest number of empty boxes.
3. Count the numbers to discover what number is missing.
4. Put the missing number in the empty box.
5. Make sure the number fits in both the row and column!
   REMEMBER: A NUMBER CAN APPEAR ONLY ONCE IN EACH
   ROW AND COLUMN!!

Do you remember how to get started on this one? Remember make a plan
BEFORE working on this page.

	1	5	4	2
5		4		1
1	2	3	5	
4	5		1	3
	4	1		5

You are getting this!

144

Do you remember how to get started on this one? Remember BEFORE working on this page, make a plan.

1	3		4	2
3			2	5
4	2		5	1
2	5	1		
5	4		1	

THIS CHALLENGE USES A NEW STRATEGY! BE CAREFUL!

		3	4	1
		5	2	4
2	1	4		
3	4	2	1	5
4	5		3	2

There is an additional step to this challenge! After completing strategy # 3 you will find the block of 4 empty boxes in the left corner needs a different strategy. Looking across you see the numbers 3, 4, and 1. This means a 2 & a 5 are missing. Now look down the first column and there is a 2, 3, & 4. So, that column already has a 2 so there is only one possible number that can go there. What is it? (If student is not sure, ask "Would it be a 2 or a 5? Remember, there already is a 2 in that column". After answers 5, continue with..) So now the first row has a five, empty box, 3, 4, and 1. What is needed to complete that row?....Now you can finish completing this challenge.

Before you start tell me the strategy.

1	2			4
5	3			1
4	1	3	2	
		4	1	3
		1	5	2

USE THE SAME STRATEGY YOU USED ON THE PREVIOUS
CHALLENGE TO SOLVE THIS ONE!

Do this the same way. The number of empty boxes continue to increase but if you follow the strategy you will never be lost. Always begin by counting before you start filling in the boxes.

	2	5	3	1
1	4	3	2	5
	5	2	1	4
5	3	1	4	

		3	2	5
3		5	4	1
1		4		2
5		2		
2		1	3	4

ALWAYS COUNT FIRST. MAKE A PLAN BEFORE YOU START!

2		5	4	
		4		3
			5	4
1	4		3	5
4	5	3		2

Tell me your plan first.

	2	5	4	1
2			1	5
5			2	4
1	4	2		
4	5	1		

4	2	5		
5		1	2	4
			4	5
2	5		1	
	4	3		2

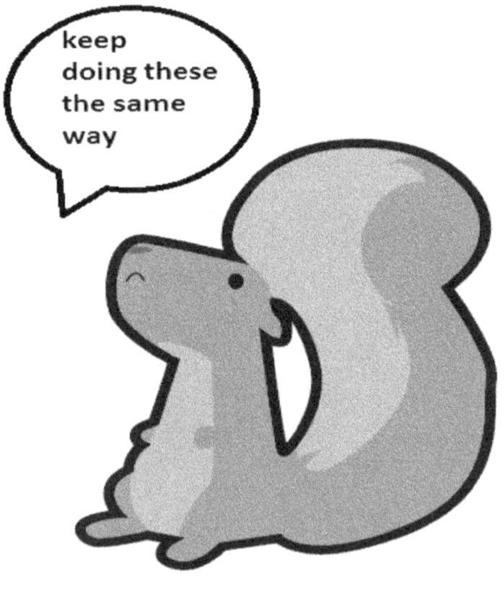
keep
doing these
the same
way

How about this one? **Look-count-think**… what is missing—then fill in the empty boxes!!

	3		2	5
		5	1	4
	5	1		3
	4		3	1
	1	3	5	

KEEP GOING!!!

5	3	4		
	2		3	1
			4	
3	4	1		5
2			5	4

	3		1	
3		5	4	2
	5	2		1
5		1	2	
	2		5	4

3		4		5
4	1		3	
2		1		3
	3		5	
	4	3		1

			1	2
3	5			4
5	1		4	
1		4	3	
2	4			1

	5	4	3	
4		5		3
2	1		4	
5		1		4
	4	2	5	

2		5		
	1		3	5
3		1	5	
	5	4		3
5	2		4	

3	5	4		
1	2			4
5			4	
		3	5	1
		1		5

This one is different because there is more than one solution. Take your time and you will get it correct!

5		4		2
3		5		1
2		1		3
4		2		5
1		3		4

NOW IT IS YOUR TURN!

First put numbers in each square so that there is not the same number in
any row or column.

Next, copy the numbers in the box below, but leave three or four of the boxes blank.

NOW...ask your guide to try to figure out your puzzle. Be sure to tell them the steps in order to do it correctly.

YOU FINISHED THE FIRST PART OF LEVEL 4 AND CAN GO TO THE YELLOW MANUAL!

LEVEL 5

FOR THE GUIDE

This level has 6 rather than 5 numbers which increases the number of boxes to 36. With this many boxes it is important that strategies learned from the previous levels be internalized and ready for use by the student (and guide). Before beginning this level the five steps for success should be reviewed. For the student to maximize benefits from this level, the guide must be familiar with the strategies, the key or solutions to each challenge, as well as be able to gradually but consistently, fade out the scaffolding.

Sustained attention is stretched on this level because time to develop and implement a strategy increases substantially. There should be plenty of opportunities for the guide to be interactive, supportive and stress the use of a consistent approach to each challenge.

Memory is also stretched because the strategies for mastery must be retained while the sequence in the challenge is considered. The guide needs to encourage taking time for planning/problem-solving. However, there has to be continued progress toward completion of each challenge. Should the student appear to become unsure of the next step, a prompt like "Where are you?" or "Share with me what options/strategies you have" or "Think aloud so we can work together on these" should assist in the problem-solving process.

REMEMBER: IT IS O.K. IF A LEVEL IS NOT COMPLETED DURING EACH SESSION!!!

The goal is 100% success. For that to occur, the amount of prompting required will vary by student. This is an example of the student and instructor creating the environment where the "Construction zone" in the zone of proximal development is addressed and learning is taking place.

The guide is encouraged to work with the student in discovering related situations in the student's life when using strategies might be used for a successful outcome. Should the student not be able to think of any, the guide should assist by brainstorming and developing strategies for various situations in the student's academic and social life. Examples include: preparing for school, keeping desk organized, doing math problems, reading for content, doing homework, completing chores. This is where graphic organizers, organizational skills, or writing steps to completing math problems will overlap with classroom curriculum.

LEVEL 5

	2	3	4	5	6
2		6	3	1	4
3	4	2		6	1
4	6	1	2	3	5
5	1	4	6	2	
6	3	5	1	4	2

2	3	1	5	6	4
	6	4	3	1	2
3	5		4	2	1
6	4	2		3	5
4	1	3	2	5	6
1	2	5	6	4	

2	6	1	4	5	3
	1	4	5	3	2
4	5		3	1	6
1	4	3	2		5
5	3	6	1	2	4
3	2	5	6	4	

6	1		3	5	2
	5	3	6	1	4
3	2	6		4	1
4	6	2	1	3	5
5		1	2	6	3
1	3	5	4		6

170

	1	3	6	5	4
3		6	2		1
1	4	2	3	6	
5	6	1		3	2
6	2		5	1	3
4		5	1	2	6

1	6		3	5	4
4	5	6	2	1	
2	4	3		6	1
	2	1	4	3	6
3	1	4	6		
6	3	5	1	4	

3	2	1		5	
6	1	4	5		2
	4	3	6	2	5
2	5		3	1	4
5	6	2	1	4	
4		5	2		1

6	1	4		5	2
2	5	3	6	1	4
3	2	6	5		1
4	6	2			5
1		5	2	6	
	3		4	2	6

	1	6	4	5	2
2	5		6	1	4
4	3	2	5		1
6		4	1	3	5
5	4		3	2	6
	6	5		4	

4	1	6	3	5	
		4	2	3	1
5	2		1	4	6
3	6		4	1	
	4	1		6	3
1	3	5	6		4

176

5	1	4	3		6
4		6		1	3
	2		5	4	1
3	6		1	5	4
	4	1		3	
	1 3	5	4		2

3	2	1		5	
	5		3	2	4
6		2	5		1
2		3	6	4	5
4	6			1	3
5	3	4	1		

	1	4		5	6
6	4	5			3
	2		6	4	1
1	3	2		6	
		1	2	3	5
3	5	6	4	1	

2	1	3	6		
3		6	2	4	
1		2			5
5	6	1	4	3	2
6		4	5	1	
	3		1	2	6

2	6		4	5	3
		4	5	3	
4	5		3		6
1	4		2	6	5
5	3	6			4
3		5	6	4	

5	6	1		2	4
2			1		
1	2		4	5	
	1	4	5	6	2
6	4		2		1
	3	2	6	1	5

YEAH!!!!!

YOU FINISHED THIS PORTION OF LEVEL 5 AND CAN GO TO THE YELLOW BOOKLET TO COMPLETE THAT LEVEL 5!!

Just keep your thinking hat on and you will do great!!!

LEVEL 6

FOR THE GUIDE

This Level continues with 6 numbers and 36 boxes. The strategies remain the same. However, the complexity of the challenges increases. In spite of the increase in difficulty, the student should continue experiencing success because of the practice from the previous Level. Practice, or rehearsal, is as important in cognitive development as it is in any athletic or academic skills. The important objective is to remember the process, not just solve the challenge. From time to time, it would be good to ask the student "What is your strategy?" or "What are you doing?" This will assist in keeping the problem-solving on a conscious level. At times, the student should be reminded to "think aloud" so that both the student and guide hear the problem-solving process. Many students put their thought process on "cruise control" which increases the likelihood of errors. The on-going reminders keep the process between student and guide working in tandem increasing the ability to continue conscious planning.

Before beginning this level the five steps need to be reviewed because the steps to solving these challenges remain similar to previous levels. For the student to maximize benefits from this level, the guide must be familiar with the strategies, the key to each challenge as well as be able to gradually, but consistently, fade out the scaffolding.

A number of cognitive skills are further developed as this Level is completed. *Sustained attention* is stretched on this level because time to develop and implement a strategy increases substantially. There should be plenty of opportunities for the guide to be interactive, supportive and stress the use of a consistent approach to each challenge. *Memory* is further stretched because the strategies for mastery must be retained while the sequence in the challenge is considered. For some students it is difficult to keep the various concepts on the level of conscious planning. This level was partially designed with those in mind. Even though the tasks are cumbersome, solutions to the challenges can be broken down into steps small enough to be solvable. *Planning/problem-solving* becomes much more important during this Level. While the student is encouraged to be methodical, there has to be continued progress toward completion of each challenge. Should the student appear to become confused, a prompt like "Where are you?" or "Share with me what options/strategies you have" or "tell me what you are thinking so we can work together on these".

REMEMBER: IT IS O.K. IF A LEVEL IS NOT COMPLETED DURING EACH SESSION!!!

Also Remember: The goal is 100% successful completion of each challenge. For that to occur, the amount of prompting required will vary by student. This is an example of the student and instructor creating the environment where the "Construction Zone" in the zone of proximal development is addressed and learning is taking place. The guide is encouraged to work with the student in discovering related situations in the student's life when planning problem-solving, strategies might be used for a successful outcome. Should the student not be able to think of any, the guide is encouraged to by brainstorming and developing strategies for various situations in the student's academic and social life.

186

LEVEL 6

	2		4	5	
2		6	3	1	4
3	4	2		6	1
4	6	1	2	3	5
5	1	4	6	2	
6	3	5	1	4	2

2	3	1	5	6	4
	6	4	3	1	2
3	5		4	2	1
6	4	2		3	5
		3	2	5	6
		5	6	4	

2	6	1	4	5	3
	1	4	5	3	2
4	5		3		
1	4	3	2		
5		6	1	2	4
3	2	5	6	4	

6	1		3	5	2
	5	3			
	2	6		4	1
4	6	2	1	3	5
5		1	2	6	3
1	3	5	4		6

	1			5	4
3					1
1	4	2	3	6	
5	6	1		3	2
6	2		5	1	3
4		5	1	2	6

1	6		3	5	4
4	5	6	2	1	
2	4	3		6	1
	2	1		3	6
3	1	4			
	3	5		4	

3	2	1		5	
6	1				2
	4			2	5
2	5		3	1	4
5	6	2	1	4	
4		5	2		1

6	1	4		5	2
2	5	3	6	1	4
3					
4	6	2			5
1		5	2	6	
	3		4	2	6

	1	6	4	5	2
2			6	1	4
4	3	2			1
6		4	1	3	5
5			3	2	6
		5		4	

4	1	6	3	5	
		4			1
5	2				6
3	6		4	1	
		1		6	3
1	3	5	6		4

5	1		3		6
4		6		1	3
	2		5	4	
3	6		1	5	4
		1			
	1 3	5	4		2

197

	2	1		5	
	5		3	2	4
		2	5		1
2		3	6	4	
4	6			1	3
5	3	4	1		

	1			5	6
6	4	5			3
	2		6	4	1
1	3	2		6	
			2	3	
3	5		4	1	

		3	6		
		6	2	4	
1		2			5
5		1	4	3	
6		4	5		
	3		1	2	6

2	6		4		
		4	5		
4	5		3		6
1			2	6	5
5	3				4
3		5	6	4	

5	6	1		2	
2			1		
1	2		4	5	
	1	4		6	2
6					1
	3	2	6		5

YEAH!!!!!

YOU FINISHED THIS PORTION OF
LEVEL 6 AND CAN GO TO LEVEL 6 IN
THE YELLOW BOOKLET!!

Just keep your thinking hat on and you
will do great!!!

LEVEL 7

FOR THE GUIDE

Due to the presence of 49 boxes in each challenge on this level, the strategies for successful completion change. It is probable, that without working closely with your student, frustration may interfere with success. The strategy leading to success will be demonstrated using the first challenge.

1. An examination of the first row shows two empty boxes with the numbers "5" and "7" missing. The obvious solution is entering "5" in the first empty box with the "7" in the second box. However, a strategy which will be incredibly useful through this level is to write the numbers "5" and "7" in the lower right hand corner of both empty boxes on that row. This will immediately provide you with both options without having to remember them as you work through the possible solutions.

2. Having completed the first and moving to the second row one sees that the numbers "4" and "5" are missing. Once more, write both numbers in the lower right hand corner of both empty boxes. Looking down the column of the first empty box, one sees a "5" already in that column. Therefore, the "4" has to fit in that box leaving only the "5" to fit in the second empty box.

3. The third row has three empty boxes with the numbers "1", "2", and "6" missing. By entering these three numbers in the lower right hand corner of each empty box, all possible options are visible. One can readily see that the "1" and "2" are directly above the first empty box leaving only the "6" as a solution. The second empty box has a "2" which means that, since the "6" has already been used, only the "1" will complete the pattern. This leaves on the "2" for the third empty box for that row.

4. Row four has only one empty box so the solution has to be "3".

5. Row five has two empty boxes and needs a "1" and a "7". Once again, placing both missing numbers in each empty box on that row helps visualize the fact that the correct number to be placed in that box is a "7". This leaves the "1" for placement in the remaining box on that row.

6. Similar to a couple of other rows, there are two numbers missing on row six – "2" and a "4". One can now easily see that the "2" is needed for the first box because there is already a "4" in that column. This, once again, leaves the remaining number for the second empty box.

7. Finally, row seven has two empty boxes and missing a "1" and a "2". By placing both of these numbers in the lower right hand side of each box immediately reveals that the "2" goes in the first box with the "1" in the second box.

NOW FOLLOW THE SAMPLE OVER THE NEXT SEVEN PAGES!!!

Sample

1. An examination of the first row shows two empty boxes with the numbers "5" and "7" missing. The obvious solution is entering "5" in the first empty box with the "7" in the second box. However, a strategy which will be useful through this level is to write the numbers "5" and "7" in the lower right hand corner of both empty boxes on that row. This will show you both choices without having to remember them as you work through the challenge.

1	2	3	4	5/7	6	5/7
2	1			6	7	3
3			7	4		5
4	5	2	1	7		6
5	3		6		4	2
6	7	5		3	1	
7	4	6	3		5	

SAMPLE (CONTINUED)

2. Moving to the second row you see that the numbers "4" and "5" are missing. Once more, write both numbers in the lower right hand corner of both empty boxes. Looking down the column of the first empty box, one sees a "5" already in that column. Therefore, the "4" has to fit in that box leaving only the "5" to fit in the second empty box.

1	2	3	4		6	
2	1	4/5	4/5	6	7	3
3			7	4		5
4	5	2	1	7		6
5	3		6		4	2
6	7	5		3	1	
7	4	6	3		5	

SAMPLE (CONTINUED)

3. The third row has three empty boxes with the numbers "1", "2", and "6" missing. By entering these three numbers in the lower right hand corner of each empty box, all possible solutions are visible. One can readily see that the "1" and "2" are directly above the first empty box leaving only the "6" as a solution. The second empty box has a "2" which means that, since the "6" has already been used, only the "1" will complete the pattern. This leaves on the "2" for the third empty box for that row.

1	2	3	4	5	6	7
2	1	4	5	6	7	3
3	1/2/6	1/2/6	7	4	1/2/6	5
4	5	2	1	7		6
5	3		6		4	2
6	7	5		3	1	
7	4	6	3		5	

SAMPLE (CONTINUED)

4. Row four has only one empty box so the solution has to be "3". Put the three where it should be.

1	2	3	4	5	6	7
2	1	4	5	6	7	3
3	6	1	7	4	2	5
4	5	2	1	7		6
5	3		6		4	2
6	7	5		3	1	
7	4	6	3		5	

SAMPLE (CONTINUED)

5. Row five has two empty boxes and needs a "1" and a "7". Putting both missing numbers in each empty box on that row helps you see that the correct number to be placed in that box is a "7". This leaves the "1" for placement in the remaining box on that row.

1	2	3	4	5	6	7
2	1	4	5	6	7	3
3	6	1	7	4	2	5
4	5	2	1	7	3	6
5	3	1/7	6	1/7	4	2
6	7	5		3	1	
7	4	6	3		5	

SAMPLE (CONTINUED)

6. There are two numbers missing on this row – "2" and "4". You see that the "2" is needed for the first box because there is already a "4" in that column. This leaves the number "4" for the second empty box.

1	2	3	4		6	
2	1	4	5	6	7	3
3	6	1	7	4	2	5
4	5	2	1	7	3	6
5	3	7	6	1	4	2
6	7	5		3	1	
			2/4			2/4
7	4	6	3		5	

SAMPLE (CONTINUED)

7. Row seven has two empty boxes and is missing a "1" and a "2". By placing both of these numbers in the lower right hand side of each box helps you see that the "2" goes in the first box with the "1" in the second box.

1	2	3	4	5	6	7
2	1	4	5	6	7	3
3	6	1	7	4	2	5
4	5	2	1	7	3	6
5	3	7	6	1	4	2
6	7	5	2	3	1	4
7	4	6	3	1/2 5	1/2

NOW TRY THIS ONE!!!

1	2	3	4		6	
2	1			6	7	3
3			7	4		5
4	5	2	1	7		6
5	3		6		4	2
6	7	5		3	1	
7	4	6	3		5	

4	2	3		5		7
	7		6		2	3
	1	4	7		3	5
7	5		4	3	1	
1	3	6	5		4	2
3	6	5		1	7	4
6	4		3	2		1

	5		7	1	2	4
1		6	5	7	4	3
7	1		6	4	3	
	6	5	4		1	7
5		4		3	6	2
	4		3	5		
4		7	2	6	5	1

	1	3	7	5	4	
3		2	6			7
	6	5	4		3	1
5		4		6	1	
4				3	6	2
1	3	6	5		2	
6	2	1	3	4	7	5

3	4	1	7	5	2	
	5	3	1	4		2
1	2	4	5		3	7
	7			3	1	
5		6			4	3
2	6	5		1	7	4
	3	7	4	2		1

7	6		1	2		3
4	7	1		3	2	5
	1	7	4		3	
3		5	7	6		4
1		6	5	7		
	5			4	7	1
5		2	3		6	7

6		3	1	2		7
	5	1		7	2	
4	1		7		3	5
				1		
1		6	5		4	2
	2	5	3	1	6	4
2						1

	2	3	5		6	7
1	4		6	7		3
6				2	3	5
7		2		3	1	6
5	3		1	6	4	
2			3			4
3	7	6	2			1

1	7	3		5	6	
5	3		6		2	1
3		1	7	2		
	5	4	2	3	1	
	1	2	5	6		
6		5	3		7	4
2	4			7	5	

	4	2		5	6	
2	1	5		7	3	
1	3		7		2	
4			2	6	1	
	7	1	5		4	
5	2	3		1		
	6	4	3		5	

6	5	3		7	2	4
7		1			4	
2	1	5			3	7
	7			6		5
5	2			3		
1		6		5	7	
4	3	7		1	5	

2	5	3		4		
5	6	4		7		2
	4	5		1		7
3	7	2		5		
7	2			3		6
4			7		5	3
	3		4		2	5

4		3	5	6	7	
1			3	5		6
3		4			5	
5		2	1		6	
	5		7	3		2
7	1	5		2		4
	3		4		1	

3		4		6	7	
4	3		2		5	6
7	6			5	4	2
	7	2	3	4		
2			7	3	1	4
6		5			3	7

2		4		6		3
6	3		2		5	4
5		2		3	6	1
3	2		5	4	1	
	4	5		7		
7		3	6		4	5

229

	5	4	2		1	
5			4		3	7
	4	6		5		2
2	7		5	4	6	
4		1		3		6
		5	3		2	4
1				2	4	

Take your time and think. This challenge can be solved.

1	3		4		2	6
	4	3	5			
4		1		6	7	
5	7				3	4
2			7	4		
		4		7		5
	2	5	1	3	4	

	2		4		6	
2	1			6	7	
3			7	4		5
	5	2	1	7		
5	3		6		4	2
6		5		3	1	
7	4		3		5	

	1		7	5	4	
3		2	6			7
	6		4		3	1
5		4		6		
4				3	6	2
1		6	5		2	
	2	1		4		5

YEAH!!!!!

YOU FINISHED LEVEL 7 AND THIS MANUAL!!!

YOU FINISHED!!! OUTSTANDING!! YOU ARE A GREAT THINKER!!

Just keep your thinking hat on and you will do great!!!